Glass Harmonica

Glass Harmonica

Geoff Bouvier

Quale Press

Special thanks to the editors of the following journals where these works first appeared: *American Poetry Review, Barrow Street, Berkeley Poetry Review, Boston Review, Conduit, Dead Horse Review, Denver Quarterly, Front Porch, Goodfoot, GutCult, Iowa Review, jubilat, La Petite Zine, LIT, MiPOesias, New American Writing, Octopus, Omnidawn Blog, Sal Mimeo, Sentence* and *Unpleasant Event Schedule.*

Cover and interior design by Kristen Sund

Front cover image courtesy of the Library of Congress (Benjamin Franklin, letter to Biambatista Beccaria, ca. 1776). Back cover image from *A descriptive catalogue of the musical instruments in the South Kensington museum, preceded by an essay on the history of musical instruments* (1874)

ISBN: 978–1–935835–03–5
LCCN: 2011930686

Quale Press
www.quale.com

Contents

II

Glass Harmonica

"Glass harmonicas belong to the family of autophone rubbed instruments. The glasses start vibrating according to a relaxation principle: when a finger rubs a bowl, it alternately catches and releases. This creates a series of impulses which set the bowl into vibration. The phenomenon is complex, so the master glass-blower needs the greatest skill to give the instrument its own character. A number of parameters can play a part, modifying the tone, the mode and the harmonic composition of the bowls. Thus, two bowls giving the same note will have different timbres according to the materials used, their shape, their thickness, their dimensions, and any hidden defects."

—Thomas Bloch, *The Glass Harmonica* (2001)

"It is true that [the Glass Harmonica] has strange effects on people. If you are irritated or disturbed by bad news, by friends or even by a disappointing lady, abstain from playing, it would only increase your disturbance."

—J.C. Miller, *Method to Teach Yourself [Glass Harmonica]* (1788)

I

Emancipation Approximation

Have you heard? The machines whirr... *Ahem.*

Some hum along, go, go choral during chores. Till idle tittle-tattle relates: someone else is it!

Out, out, wherever you are! As we rest inch locked in local traffic.

At least wind's direct. Skylines — swart hordes, jutting high stacks — intermit smoke. Mid replica and replica, populous, inhabiting the ad hoc, many seek to hide.

Me? I'm available, out on the road.

Travel Arrangements

Down, down the opening road, and away by either blurred side pull two passive, golden fields. So hold on fast, tilted into sun-squint, trunk full of stuff, cracked window whistling a tremolo. In between songs, "The alternative alternative," sanctions the radio.

Easygoing Outburst

Out on our own now, we've inhabited lots of lots lots less developed than we'd have liked. Childhood prepared some, but others can't land, like stunt planes just gassed enough to go up and turn stunts.

Only a question, but didn't the past promise pearls? (That oyster-world.) Or was it an earth betrothed? (Spoken by one whom one could've been were one a loved one.)

It's as if what left left what was once called a heaven constellated into coincidences. *Sigh.*

If I sound concerned, and like it's nighttime, and like I'm looking up — away from light pollution — and still can't see enough, then I may seem to have taken on the tone of an ex-fiancée's defiance. Why? For want of an ifless, thenless love, of a love-regardless, that's why.

Lost Prophet's Song

Call us Qualms. We want new psalms. Our ears are to shells, the shells are to the ground, but it's ground, ground, all the way down.

We're Qualms. To us, the world's a maelstrom tossing niceties. Indiscriminately, and more precisely. From foot to foot we shift: apocalypse / recovery.

Are those lives we've led? Each of us expects to end up pretty dead. We think the meantime takes up, what, slack? For distraction, we define our physiques.

Descended from condemning lines of Qualms, we're slight. Simplistic variations on allotted vocabularies. Our position becomes this: perfectly stationary.

That's "Qualm." Made of pain and bad fight. Instead of the pain part, we follow the loudest advice. Can't see what it means, but what it says seems right.

There's a name to fortify yet remedy. It's "Qualm!" At podium-sonority. Our fury is boredom-fury. Who wants to make a million-dollar bet? Postponement is what we've got left.

Phantom Pantoum

Begin?

Refrain. Begin again.

Refrain?

Go on. Again, a song.

Alone?

Go on, a song alone; then sing again with me along.

And then?

Just silence. Listen. Rest together, sitting tight. After, we may rest together silent sitting tight.

Just listen, then? Begin?

Begin.

Uplifted, Unbeaten

You, heart. Thumping happy, happy as though numb or you can't hear me.

Did I catch you correctly? Do you say a name, secretly?

Never still. As though you told, and will tell. But it reads as one tone and one gesture.

I think I understand.

It takes a lifetime to answer?

Sneaking Through The Ward?
Or Being Considerate Through The Ward

Tiptoe — hush, now — stealth becomes the early way. Characteristically we lay bare nerves against a Braille world. Dot-by-letter dares revealing then: imaginary sentences with real words in them.

We're up, it's dawn, sadly half-spent (haply half-earned?), approximately gray. Everything, this season's weather: grasp-and-go today. New and old, latest sun and undone dew, exchange a mist-and-fog, *"Hello."*

And so, well, quiet, is it? Yes. Between the distance and the windowscreen, a many-handed shower touches down, slanted freshet. Rainfall brushes grasses; drizzle presses houses; water lets us eavesdrop, runs adrift, and comes aground. All clean.

Put a finger on it. Does the rain say? Or seem to say, *"The world would be clear to you. It even writes you when it has to."*

Between Sounds, A Sense

I'd set up shop — at just the right spot — in the hallway in my house where two clocks blended talks: one ticked the other's tock. There, then, equally frequently, the moment reflected the dueling of syllables, like a trap had been clicking.

Clicking open? Clicking shut?

Clicking open? Clicking shut?

Both foremost and seconded, their questions might prove lasting. Going either way, with each clock asking.

Things Good In Themselves

Sometimes questions left for us lie around bright rooms and we ask them without question. Sometimes, no questions come: dampened rooms, straight and tidied to exclusion. And sometimes when they're delivered — defiant, inspired — among the clutter, what we ought to ask may seem encoded for another.

Stay calm; those are signs. Work hard; that's the code.

A Necessary Distance

Seizing words, from events, through a pen, for this page, in some café called Consequence. Now lines in life contend to advance, drawn from the verge where they'll distantly vanish.

A blond boy tall as the tables totters to one wall and stops. Tours to trot again. This woman whose face is an experience removes and admires her ring.

Is it ever time?

Can anyone learn to read that kind of sign?

When the boy wears a smile, I don't mind inquiring. But the woman tries — no — her gesture's foretelling, betraying its intending: I turn before her eyes can catch my eyes.

Not gazing, writing.

Refining Villanelle

When you converse with cultured repose, the impulse arises to babble or drone. But you settle on speaking appropriate prose.

Rough mouths and jaded edges persist in some facts of society's form, though people converse with cultured repose. Under spiffy syntax and unwrinkled closure there's impressive tension, seething danger, as though a bomb... Yet we settle on speaking appropriate prose.

A full sentence shuffles along and shows the trained pace of the pedestrian.

When I converse with cultured repose, I can't cry out my vows and woes and work through words toward passionless "om." I settle. In appropriate prose, who sings one's self, or even unfamiliar tones, chatting simple sense and what's outwardly known?

When people converse with cultured repose, they've settled on speaking appropriate prose.

Desired Reversal

What I wanted, I wanted so close, I consumed it. Mm. But then it wasn't my thing anymore. It was part of me, becoming my energy.

What I didn't want, I wanted so far away that I blocked it. I locked it in a site I could forget about. But now that thing consumes me, feeding back through the walls like fire, noise, or gravity.

In The Neighborhood — Infinite Distances

—inside—a bee—my window—butting—this time—this time
—this time—

Elevation

All day Sunday sings, all day Sunday vaults and sings: day music, day gracious, day easy, day dancing, a day of the sun, a day of beach's ether, a day of the day for tonight in the bowl of the sky, perhaps, for my friends and myself. We drink, become as one voyager, eat of the palm frond, party, and we party.

Until a voltage of the purified, voltage alive in inebriated air, and we're ready for others come open from liquor, to undeclare the closings of previous beliefs.

And if you emerged, and you declared, and I declared, and we declared, until our shuttle brimmed and boiled, laying claims, contending vigorous...

And if you emerged, and you and I, and you and I, and we and we, until we versed the pages with an everlasting breath...

Then in the morning, party over, full again of our powers, we'd inventory, effort-free, the speaking parts of birds and flowers.

Or night into Sunday may sing instead, night, night into Sunday may sing, vault and sing: night sighs, night swoons, night fires, night dances, night of night for the moon, night of night for the question, "Why?" Night of party of night for immaculate white of the holes in the black of the bowl of the sky.

One-Way Ticket

We're off to hit the atmosphere with utmost fears exhausted, no returns considered, no reentry needed. To leave and leave on incredible credit — each released from the lease, right at home out of place. Goodbye ideas, so long, long face.

Spinning wayward through the formerly onward, disorienting gloriously, unmeasured like nonsense on vastness, ecstatic—looking back on that massive endowment, the earth — her now expressionless raiment of cloud — radiant...

Instead, our muse the void has offered up her formless curve — an immaterial body for as-if-etched words — and she moves us even as we move, on course with love, that slant of save, in which we must believe.

Woman-Shaped Women

Ladies whose hobby's horses. Equestriennes, you'd call them. Pleasingly tapered and untapered and tapered again. But after a few of those, mere boredom. The apoplexy of chefs.

Then turning over a new... to get her together. Ah, yes. I knew the leaf of which they speak.

If I Were A Different Letter

I might be Q, the enigmatic figure proper, an O with an out, kickstood. A balloon robustly holding in its would-be-piercing pin: the letter that needs another, making one sound alone but no word without you.

Can You See A Sign If I Can't?
I See You're Significant

You're not an island, as who is. More like, we're spits, or peninsulas.

Nevertheless, when the high tide strands us — a long way — we can always sound out to where the other harbors fondness.

Shallow water ports are hard to come by, it's true, but low tide will define, and anyway the best part's inland — less wind — more there to see.

If you're headed this way, down the strait, or on the morning ferry, and we meet up somewhere a few words from here, we'd better be ready for things beautiful and strange. I'm just saying. Everything celebrates that celebrates a we-change.

A Specific Instance Of Us

Autumn moments lend the memory. In another weather, in that red car. On a lark, the two of us. Leaves remarked raucous mosaics.

Drove to an overlook, blink. Wasn't that the trailhead? And on the left, escarpments! Animated streambeds lacked walkable banks. Look at this peculiar orange mushroom, you said. Composures collecting on moss-thick rocks.

Ultimately, waterfalls, and out of them misted rainbows. Two yellow apples as a fond reward, cores over the falls. Seems we both earned scrape-like purplish souvenirs. *Goodbye, spot where we sat.*

Hiking out for hot dogs, vanilla ice cream from a truck. Funny how together all day we'd become a touchy subject.

Meek Epic

Two separate indentations on the bedcover.
　　Dark streets harvesting light rain.
　　Dumb skin.
　　Snowdrifts uncurled in spring's arms.
　　A half-kiss, a ki-.
　　Even trees inconsistently.

From The Scribbled Addenda

The surface of the lake was almost perfect, like a blue plate. No wind, nothing to upset it. You told me you wanted to break the lake. Why would you want to break the lake?

Well full of wonder down an autumn's early lightfall pretending, we lapsed in a copse, then, panting. Along an owed series of ifs that thenned together in no wind out of mind...

I loved you past tense, beyond tense.

Lakeside, we were dream defiers, dream deifiers. Forget the debts. Forget the evening chill. There was nothing we needed to get through our heads.

Between us, I too wanted to break the lake. To reset it more perfect.

Black And White,
And The Grey Gray Thing

We were two to a tee, yea, we were woe. Needed an inordinate amount of mint in it, or else the status was staleness. Trusted tenses, though they'd trussed us. And hoped what one'd done'd add up to elation, earned. Aligned by better ends' means.

Meantime, meanness. The thickest thickset thickets.

I'm Like An Irate Pirate. It's Like This.

Love acquired and requited acquitted us. In fits and starts, and free to stall, we fell to razing complex edifices.

What ho!

That garden had variety. Even periodic shore-marshaled whooshes echoing off bluffs.

We could've stopped traffic. Instead we chased ducks.

It Got Late And Deep In Snow

You left, like handedness or a shoe.

Till We Overcome Minutiae And Inertia

Was the old cause a placebo? Nothing's taken an effect.

What with workweeks walking off daydaydaydayday, like concrete poems where Sky Bruiser bullies pink brick adobe abodes, and Multitudinous Tide exhales, as we speak, banalities breathed without check. Tuneless, ceaseless, askless words.

Let the lies of the loudest bird be heard!

This Care Case We Carry Pain In, Apace

Pigeons'll still sit and shit on the sill. Tides'll go on ripening. In defense of not facing, been defacing the fencing. Finding refuge in a room attuned to silence and to sound.

From a locked and almost airless chest: new feelinglocations. Same old heartolalia.

Word Travels

Sociable trees, for instance, angle up through chatty wind, that shifty friend, who breathes three seasons through the trees' leaves, which blush. When they fall, fast, it's out of confidence — giving us up to curious grass.

Nature can't help herself, publicizing private alibis.

Even pacified ocean passages drift our information, signing along wide shorelines openly, naming bad tidings. And if that weren't faithless prose enough, the deep condenses into clouds and drops, till intimate wordings inland cover eaves. In short, voluminous seas — those saying most — must learn secrets last.

So the stars, then? The stars?

What else might silently forget our fatal details every night?

Better Foreign Policy

Torn, a tear descends...
>   Whose tear?
>   Property's unimportant here. A tear's a tear.

Retired To The Tropics

Down there, only sun on sand — a torrid, emptied air. No wetted middle space's dins accomplish, leaved and buzzing, birded lushly, flush with green good life.

Granted, we could've stayed and learned the strident signs. Instead we stole our own ways out here, far, and left whatever singing things we could. (Whatever it was they said…)

Near and soon, purple deepens dusk the same. Though no repetitious crickets gush their thanks thanks thanks thanks thanks be to moon. The single season tightens tuned along a few degrees of weathered string.

Those Old Familiar Ditties

The sound of wind in trees with leaves that move, I overheard. Then I moved and hit my final height, and westward southward fronds had dropped the song.

The stopped winds let me sing alone. No tone, not one. A long forgotten tune.

Instead... instead...

What was it said, what says, and why did I, so sudden, ever hear that word *instead*? (And if it never happened once, it does, this time, instead.)

Instead, strict issuing vow, a quieter wind that gathers in the years has fanned a ready, waiting mind, mine, and that moves now.

In Focus

Sobering moment — this evening sun's gone down. So be it.

Twilight shows our broken world's all right. Reminds us once in early morning, once this time of almost night. Otherwise, a blue noon reveals, as blackest nighttime hides, too much. Otherwise, these upward things — power lines, roof eaves, traffic lights, the trees — slouch in scarce relation to that sky.

Decidedly here, not there.

But now — as with morning's shallow blackness coming blue — now — as evening deepens, going blueness out to black — two interludes a day — maybe twenty-minute phases either way — our upward things turn upright things.

Ground and sky, justify.

Nested

Cityscape nested in a sconce of night.

What I meant, was. No presence for the unintended. We'd earned our lives and they'd taken to us. Felt complicit in a shift and grew, then, then shed superfluous wings.

I can't remember the morning I first woke up to a day that wasn't pure improvisation. But I did. And now my hours play through themes and plans I have to try for to fulfill.

Out there, the totality of weighed effects balances one half of things: teeter. The unsaid other half in here pulls its weight and holds its own, and has us (almost) level: totter.

It's Always Right There

—slow and free, negotiating patiently—crossing us, in fact, with ominous tracks, coming for to carry—

A Glass Harmonica's Last Song

Ptsh

II

No Country

"Where now?" They asked. Then every other minute, "Now? Here?"

There, there. There, there. Where no one who cares hears us cry anymore.

The All-New Solar-Powered Palinode

It occurs to some poets, on their ways home: we've confused ourselves with the sun. Perhaps our solace came from gazing too long at cloudless solipsism.

Not to imply our star who art on high is self-absorbed, nor that The Daymaker's just another working light along a relative line of lights, although each of these ideas pass as meaningful and plausible.

Down here, sporty Echoes, red Accents, used Eclipses, souped up Legends, and huge-if-inefficient Expeditions, each in independent fits and starts, abut.

But again, at some point, that old sun's going to set. And most of us will still be out, on grand extending starlight-like night highways, lined around the planet.

Jugglers

New schedule. Good people. Forget plans and names. The places we've lived blend into the same.

Toss it all up, hold other claims. In the air, all tossed up, it flies yet remains.

Trophies we throw, we think, "Must have belonged to me." Trinkets one catches, one flips away playfully, possessed by the fitful give-and-take between levity and gravity.

And in the end, it's just a start — a balancing, precarious gift — art — relieves the misplaced gift of the heart.

Partial To The Whole

It's always something unbalances the rest. That from another side, this about-face.

We adjust and adjust, and an admirable awareness might encompass — some grand new focus — but for every center cleared, edges blur and disappear.

Cold deepness comes, warm shallows go. For each potential yes, several possible no's.

Who can and can't live without phases and stages?

Problem Solving Elements

The clouds and seas twist out of joint. Distinguished moisture's heard. Today — rain drops — tries to set them back together. Up above, remember, remember, trembles immoderate fire.

Here, the realized strand's no compromise, for spacious beach, for transitory sands unclaimed. Beneath high, wide, unbiased clouds, in deep, all shallows swab and dab. And from the air, near-limitless promise surges, settles, drifts, and lags.

Aground, out through, and in excess of this exterior — there's hope in inland water.

Were They Wrong About The Rocks' Song?

When waves have ground them into grating each other, in the face of overwhelmingly upsweeping assertions — the ones between the shore's and the ocean's — wouldn't it be lively things rocks sing?

Other theories abound. But only animated stones make sound.

Refining Sestina

With intention, echoes echo — each repeating — disenchanted in a canyon, always changing.

Always changing with direction, in a canyon, echoes echo, disenchanted, each repeating.

Each repeating, always changing, disenchanted with expression, echoes echo in a canyon.

In a canyon, each repeating, echoes echo, always changing, with impressions, disenchanted.

Disenchanted in a canyon with inflection, each repeating, always changing, echoes echo.

Echoes echo, disenchanted, always changing in a canyon, each repeating, with corrections.

Who Knows Weather, Or Not

It could cloud. It couldn't cloud.

Symmetry Too Literally

Too symmetry.

Converse Nation

Light on your hair, like potion through a filter. Our faces in shadow. That voice...

Are you my mother?

Let's sing to each other. Indefinitely.

The one about yes in a no country.

Experts Agree

Ignorance is the root of all evil bliss. Nuclear power's nonpolluting dangerous. Sexuality is genetically determined a choice. Nature nurture is a crucial secondary factor in shaping personality. Government aid might can't save a national economy. The prison system seems effective needs improvement. People have everything little to do with the global climate. There's no chance it's a certainty that there is life on other planets. Polls are a flawed outstanding indication of who will win lose an election. Drinking while pregnant is anathema just fine in moderation. God absolutely doesn't does exist. Life begins at conception birth. Classical music merely relaxes raises IQ. Religion is hokum truth. Fluoridated water lowers hormone levels is beneficial for teeth. People are fundamentally honest corrupt. Absence makes the heart forget grow fonder. The nature of the human mind is to comply to wander. It's foolish wise to forego a seasonal flu shot. A mother should indulge ignore a crying infant. The earth is round flat. Health care is a right privilege. Enhanced interrogation techniques are unethical effective. Giving food to the poor keeps them healthy makes them lazy. Eggs can shouldn't be eaten daily. The phonic method is a bad good way to teach young children to read. Time is the enemy on your side.

The News Today

Most are disinclined to accept the surplus denial lately.

Last week, our furniture was found to have more occupations than we do.

Here's to peace in our times (on the government's terms). To being light, sweet, crude.

Ah, poverty. Always somewhere between the homepage and the back page, right when we went to forget about it.

What's wrong with offering everyone Medical Security?

We're all pretty damned unsatisfied to be wounded, and the ability to say as much must be protected.

There ought to be a Funeral Channel.

"I'll fire aimlessly if you don't come out," screamed a man with no standard to understand loneliness by.

I heard they were finally going to legalize gay.

There's a prevailing air of resolution. From the top down, the word is, "Pain never hurt anyone."

Transparent Media

We see through you.

To elucidate, you're supposed to help us see. You know, like an eyeball.

Oh. Did you think I meant you're invisible? No, the opposite. We can't help but see you, in that sense, in the sense that, like an eyeball, you encompass the view.

Or did you think I was calling you out on deceit? Well, you're the one to look through, still, though not so much the one to look to.

Take that the best way, as I do, Media. A disenhancement pill.

So So Mother Tongue

Still unsteady, understudy?

Standing by, old standby?

I kid, kid. But time might rhyme with rhyme for a reason, you think?

And waht abuot the fcat taht ftify-fvie percnet of tohse who raed Eglnsih can udnestrnad excatcly waht's wrtiten hree?

Without even having to read it again.

And then there's the other forty-five percent who'll see such sport and never understand it. Odd.

Now, from this moment, frist and lsat, let's alternate, o my alternate. Split it with you fifty-five/forty-five. Or ftory-fvie/ftify-fvie, whatever. Toward us existing in an everlasting state of harmony. Homrany. Or are you, too, too corrupted?

So far, only the dead can come for to get all carried away like this when they're interrupted.

Confident Agent

Tomorrow's ship's for sale but hasn't sailed yet, nor sold. Which sort of synchs up.

Got soul. Vital order needs rerouting. Hope'll still be at harbor, for pacification, tooting.

Today's evening's busy too, dinners will din, if to an extent uncoordinated. And so go twenty-four more of what were ours.

To make do, then, and to make do well, let's be good, for goodness' sake, and later we can still be being good.

Yesterday, I crossed from my list the iconic itinerant Item, time. Choosing laughter, you remember, the universal significance with the incomparable future.

And through a scenic science: re-minting mimetic documents, to the letter. Telling time, now, how it could be — seeing as I'm the better editor.

This Postmodern, It Play One

So. Still didn't get wind? Facts were supposed to be in.

Yeah, in *question*: de-sequestered from worn, torn couches.

And out among uninterrupted idiosyncrasies, considering: not one right angle exists in nature. Think about it. Lines and curves? Abundantly got. But the rest is our contribution. Folks's.

As for factses, the fact we can't learn new feelings proves absolutely reasonable, though perfectly disappointing. There may be distress at this felt fact, for instance: if you swum one ocean, you swum 'em all.

Ours does seem a history of cynical extrapolators.

And, and hopeful innovators!

In that skin itself is given to forget... it sloughs it off, and comes replaced. And then? We say one's skin has never swum a certain, unpacifiable ocean.

Not that much has changed. Not as much as it'll have had to have changed.

I Will Not Excuse You, You Shall Not Be Excused, Excuses Shall Not Be Admitted, There Is No Excuse Shall Serve, You Shall Not Be Excused

Culture hit pockets of chaos yesteryear, bad hair years. In most cases, responsibility fell to hot weather. Other places, criminals ate plenteous Twinkies. Magnetic fields polarized multiple apartments. Unabashed conspiratorial theorists schemed.

Look it up. Right there in the dictionary. Everyone swung as a monkey once. And some served as artist's models as kids. Anything can appear like a good idea at the time. Before wind takes it, sun hits the eyes, and whatever's in the stars alights, spins, and plays its side out.

Meantime, watch that cholesterol. And never do what's not in your job description, except for hit the snooze button. Advice from one whose inhibitions lay, finally downed. But who ages and tires learning fundamental American lessons, like: *If you want to do it, why shouldn't you?* Hmm.

Ethics? Genetics? Heavy metal music? Faugh! Testosterone, PMS — it's pretty much the same. So we've got our chemical imbalances. There's forevermore a story. Even to those who cry, appealing for higher morality.

Hell, times are tough. Death. Bad Karma. Yet it all looks terrific in commercials, explain that. In general, I'm not opposed to the experience of daylight. But then, these voices in my head, split seconds of clarity...

What I mean is, we haven't had time to iron out the bugs yet. Though a few may grow curious. And others feel fantastically lucky.

Whether or not the power cuts. Again. Or we can't come by words.

WWPD (What Would Poetry Do?)

Well, here's another fine poem you've gotten us into.

It's a poem. Honest.

Sometimes it's hard to see what all the poetry's about. As poetry would have it.

I poeticize, therefore I am. I've never met a poem I didn't like. Poetry adds life. Poems are forever. Poetry tries harder.

Poetry wants *you*. Give poems a chance. You're in good hands with poetry. A poem a day helps you work, rest, and play.

It's poetry time. Reach out and poeticize someone. Don't leave home without poems. Have a break, have a poem. Let there be poetry.

I can't believe it's not poetry. This is your brain on poetry. When in poems, you do as the poetry does. Poetry never sleeps. Poetry will tell. Poems speak louder than words. Just say poetry.

Got poetry?

A fool and his poems are soon parted. Sometimes you feel like a poem, sometimes you don't. You're barking up the wrong poem. This is only the tip of the poem.

Look what the poem dragged in. Just in the nick of poetry. Sitting there like a bump on a poem. Poetry happens. It takes a tough person to make a tender poem. Let's cut to the poetry.

Ask not what a poem can do for you, but what you can do for poetry. Let sleeping poems lie. Keep everything at poem's length. Put your best poems forward. One good poem deserves another. Poetry is everywhere you want to be.

May poetry be at your back. Like a poem in a china shop. There's more here than meets the poem. The poetry's in the details. Sometimes you can't put your poetry on it.

Never underestimate the power of a poem. Poetry is the answer.

Poetry, take me away! To poetry, and beyond!

Lay your poetry on the table. Get all your poems in a row. Put your poetry to the grindstone. Every poem has a silver lining.

Someday my poem will come. I'd walk a mile for a poem. Home is where the poetry is. The proof is in the poem.

Happier than a word in a poem. Happy-go-poetry.

In poems we trust.

You had me at "poetry."

So Why Stay Awake?

'Cause clouds glow audible, after a flashin'. Critical thinking curls at one's feet and cascades asleep.

To loll away in the soul tonight and levy a reverie, clip sedges from the edges of cells of thought-masonry. Go, and be redrawn around a blank in the mouth that can't be filled, no, although enlighteningly.

Searched The Ether And The Other; Found Neither

To those a-fluent in Feeling, and therefore not attuned to cleaner grades of Meaning, a thousand dialects object, adjoin, desist, and settle in. First period, mourning. Second period? After?

Many, many, many renovations going on. Quests. Signs that greet fixers and seekers must read, I don't know, "Can't Speak?"

Diagnoses have it: products of dredging projects. So seconds or so of spinning conjure instance, instance, instance — lighthousesque — and swathe in beam this alternately light then darkened space.

You see? It comes on but to go from us, understanding be comfortless.

Sonnet: Manidest Festiny

Where, oh where has our affect all gone? Where, oh where can it be? Yawning through tragedies, practicing catastrophic ennui.

You start off asking yourself stuff, like, do I remember the original pronunciation? But how can you have a pre-, if you don't know the dif-, or understand the re-?

One checks, and four out of five quintessences surveyed cite the point but have landed beside it. They say we're as prey in playgrounds: superficially safe, super unwitting. But I'm not terrified of the threatened clandestine predating. "My" government's attempts to make me as much notwithstanding.

Often what expands expands to just short of consonance. And when it does, it's because that's just what it does.

Which about ditches us opposite that obsolete art, opera. The one where absolute performative pitch conveyed even frivolous trivia.

Sonnet: A Heart's Content

Whatever'd moved in rated great angles. Admired a camber and inheritor's design. Comparison pointed homeward, comparison.

After fairer forests, plants enthickening, pre-pomp yet post-disgust, flocks flocked approximately appropriately. Lacks around the greening id precipitated introcircumspection.

Whoever'd find happiness in any state'd jingle coins now, not be jangled by change, even single out songs. Scarves becoming doves at time's sleight-of-behest'd become becoming to anyone who'd be anyone happy, by then. Meanwhile, three hands itch a face. And moving in the matter, what abides?

A day, each night, might park anywhere, unflappable as a beefeater. But at dawn — soon — all will be song.

(To the scarecrow's tune): "I'd put a quarter in it, and I'd keep it there a minute, if I only had a pocket."

All's Both Port And Transport

With half the light a glass admits, it reflects. At a wall a half a call returns...

Such penetrating audacity. Every surface a hollow, haunted by capacities.

Small Talk Lament

We speak the same. Languish. Shoot the breezes with half-truth.
Never mind, old heart. Race you to the absolute.

Last Laps Before Committing

Now loud cars sear near, fast, lest this be listless. Race!

Or, wait. What was the name of that revolutionary person? No, the one who turned down the existing conclusion, careering in a loud car, not far from here?

Go, loud cars, sear on, to subjects unknown.

For Our Failings, I Mean, Feelings

Once it was room temperature, thank you, and holding. Bodies hit average heights. What morning lawns were smelled, smelled mown. And memory? It welled. All those in favor with stars threw light.

Maintaining, some scored pre-mortem pills of doesn't-matter-anymore, somethingsomethamine, and dosed away the days with abandon and friends. And the nights became seamless, time impregnable, synaesthetic. No pain untended.

The Stupendous Return Of The Mesmerizing Glass Harmonica

In shards, scattered by the seats of their poetics, the muses are addressing us.

Are those you, Schizophrenia? Whispering in confidence? (Explaining (in-) (de-) cisive tones, not to mention moistened warmth.)

I'm of many womany minds...

Meantime, though, it's meaning time. A minute largely occupied with sixty second thoughts.

Past Oral (No Voices Left Of Dissent)

Spring! Out loud! Oh, oh that old urge to onomatopoeia... Or is it alliteration? Interrogation? Oh, so many old urges... And each one too elliptical for sentences to hold... Not even spoken words could ever hold...

Mother, may I?

Yes, it's May.

Patriotic showers bring us national flowers, and the wind on its errands every after-equinox evinces. Blow harder, activist! Persuade those trees. And the trees're swayed, some, but in the end just keep returning to positions.

Come dusk again against the warmer skies the inset insects, shifting, quicken. Shh. Listen. It sounds like yes. Yes? Yes. Yes? Yes.

Twenty-Six Native American Naming Events, Always Odd, Always On The Bad Side

Forgets-The-Keys, Too-Set-In-Old-Ways, Can't-Learn-Compassion, Walks-Around-Naked-With-The-Blinds-Half-Open, Talks-Big, Ogles-Possessions, Often-Unhappy-For-No-Reason, Sleeps-Excessively, Wracked-By-Insecurities, Always-Thinks-Money, Gesticulates-Wildly, Listens-With-Presumption, Hasn't-Settled, Can't-Commit, Stupid-Blurter, Doesn't-Wear-A-Seatbelt, Won't-Apologize, Unwise, Trapped-In-Bad-Habits, Never-Wants-Help, Tells-Jokes-At-Everyone-Else's-Expense, Wanton-Antagonist, Cursed-And-Might-Be-Blessed, Shortcut-Taker, Plagiarist, Too-Hard-On-Myself.

Yclept Eponymous

Was emerging dirty as I'd groped the known specifics spouting sudden words-of-mouth. A cellar door wedged off its hinge. In hearing, then, bones beneath my house removed addressed me; they taught, and I spelled them. Again and again. Out old untold grounds...

A world — arbitrary earthy nouns — won free then beyond mention. Around the turns? Uncertain dips and climbs.

They're now unnamed, but come calms, may resemble ensembles, not ignorant paucities of paths. Grace, no doubt, and hardly thinking need function. Limpid lucid lessons in tuition bathe.

The Orders Of Fire

In love with their lyrics, they'd led us by rote — lined up like ants, everyone on foot, spelled as we felt — toward a conflagration, chastening adulteration.

Songs, then — lit songs, light, long in teams — untied themselves — night stops — lashed up and snapped at the tips of bright knots — hot hopes — tied back the dark and untied from old tricks.

Sung, then — tongued aflame. To heat — re-baptized by rote.

In love with their lyrics, lost to the notes.

DayDayDayDayDay

I

Yawp! Yawp! Yawp!

Again!? Ungodly a.m. Snooze some...

Yawp! Yawp!

Snooze again?

No. Just undo it. Just say yes. Take that strengthening shower, till wafting off lathered in homeopathic *happiness*...

...angling on the edge of a fortunate premise. Yes? "Some dogs' days transcend untimely morns that bore them."

And now! In time, in lieu, and just in case, if still a smidgen out of sorts, well-dressed to ride on the excitement of uncertainty, day-bound, unloosed, it's okay. So which way?

Out the door, possessed of prosperity: plenty iffy credit for necessities, two rye toasted buttered slices, exaggerated (caffeinated) intensities.

II

On a blank check-back penning "Fee's Ode" at Don't Walk lights, your faithful broke poet bends to a streetside box: upsnap! No quarter. Only headlines via tinted glass this day.

Still seeming simultaneous, what lies out there's to be parsed, numerous humors over sidewalks mist up under heating light.

Sorry, can't tip complimentary homeless people to their caps, purple muumuued lady in the supermarket does like to chat, and dividends append with common man's appropriations outstretched.

Meantime, starts to feel quite right. Traffic trafficking, faucets faucing, awnings awning, and ants hefting body-ratios in kitchen crumbs' weights. Nothing early, nothing's late. Through drifting consciousness, decimal place.

Pursuing interim mediums and a search that is "re-." Who holds remotest control? Let's go! They're burning daylight. Tons of wills being done, tons of graces, here as elsewhere.

III

Grappling back impassive time, did take no map to be my town... short-term... Oh good o'clock! I'm off to hit the long way for a browse, avid binds propped atop abutting spines and leaning quietness' gently guided lines. For me to be mine.

After, about a flower, a hummingbird reminder... then leaves. Incessant momentousness. To justify the braes of donkey to man.

And after, every evening even seems to be extending — a swifter breeze's seeking ever softer sough — a similar, so, dispassionate temperature to the rest of us. For every pennant, flaccid standard, flagging banner, and slackened streamer: warmed embrace.

IV

Could be bliss, this, couldn't it? An all-out rush to darkness undressed, with scarce a kink or waver on the coming arcs of stardom.

And look: a bird may lay a song here, if half-safe. Watched, it might hatch. A total ellipse of the one.

Elated, I've deleted loss. Can yuk it up somewhat truculently. Wattage, I think, is what light lights for.

Later, not late, on a park bench at dusk, and, lo! "Hi."

Never to cool to less than a compassionate eye, passing by.

Space For Worn Words Unspent

Had the moon sewn to the pocket of a coat. New moon, old coat, I knew what that meant.

I've since forgot. Though now I'm warm, and keep each coin in the coat-hole-form of a new moon none can see.

Personal

Recovering lyricist seeks prosaic wind, doubtless indirection returning to send. Equal inspiration, plotted on the wing, for lively quiet telling between lapses into song.

quale [kwä-lay]: *Eng. n* 1. A property (such as hardness) considered apart from things that have that property. 2. A property that is experienced as distinct from any source it may have in a physical object. *Ital. pron.a.* 1. Which, what. 2. Who. 3. Some. 4. As, just as.

Made in United States
North Haven, CT
11 December 2021

12471510R00062